# CONTENTS

WESTERN
SAMOA

SAVAII

Apia

UPOLU

TUTUILA

Pago
Pago

EASTERN
SAMOA

VAVAU

TOFUA

TONGA
ISLANDS

Nukualofa

TONGATABU

## Locales of thirty-two full-page pictures

# let's travel in the
# SOUTH SEAS

**Edited by Darlene Geis**

A TRAVEL PRESS BOOK

PICTURE ACKNOWLEDGMENTS
The pictures and illustrations in this book were taken in the South Seas by Ewing
Krainin. For the black-and-white photographs we wish to thank Ewing Krainin; Pan
American Airways; George Holton, Erwin Lang and Frederick Ayer from Photo
Researchers, Inc.; Richard Harrington from Three Lions; United Press International
Photo; The Museum of Primitive Art of New York; and the Bettmann Archive. The
map was made by Enrico Arno.

THIRD PRINTING

Original copyright, © 1961 by Columbia Record Club, Inc., New York, N.Y.
under the title of *A Colorslide Tour of The South Seas*. All rights reserved.
New edition published 1965 by CHILDRENS PRESS, INC., Chicago.
Published simultaneously in Canada.          Lithographed in the U.S.A.
Library of Congress Catalog Card Number: 65-15979

# MAGIC ISLANDS OF
# THE SOUTH PACIFIC

A DREAM of tropical islands has haunted the imaginations of men through the ages. Even the ancients had their legend of Atlantis, a lovely and perfect island that was lost beneath the sea. The desire to escape from the civilized world and regain the pleasures of paradise on some palm-shaded isle has sent many men adventuring over distant waters.

The writers Robert Louis Stevenson, Somerset Maugham and James Michener, and the artist Paul Gauguin (*goh*-GANN) found their dusky Edens in the South Seas. They in turn, with their romantic tales and exotic paintings, have given the dream reality and have inspired others with a longing for those far-away islands. Today the green jewels that lie scattered over the dazzling blue vastness of the South Pacific still have their remote charm and their old magic, but now they can be reached quickly and in comfort by plane or ship, and thousands of tourists can savor their escapist delights.

The Pacific is a world in itself, covering nearly one-third of the total area of our planet, and its size is greater than the entire land surface of the globe. In that immensity of water, islands seemingly as countless as the stars are sprinkled—especially in the south and west. On a map they are constellations of pinpoints, each group with its own melodious name. The entire island-spangled area is known as Oceania (*oh-she*-AN-*ih-uh*), and it includes the large land masses of Borneo, Sumatra, Java and New Guinea. But it is the isolated little islands and groups cast up by volcanoes from the ocean floor, or built by generations of coral colonies, that entice us from half a world away.

## THE ISLAND PEOPLE

Not the least of the South Seas' fascination lies in its people—the bronzed Adams and golden-skinned Eves of a thousand romantic tales. Actually the South Sea Islanders fall into three main groups, each living in a different region of the Pacific and possessing different physical characteristics and speech. About 25,000 years ago the lush bits of land that dot the Pacific were uninhabited. Then in wave upon wave of remarkable migrations from Asia to the large islands and finally by

*A Samoan maiden, dressed for an ancient ceremony, personifies old Polynesia.*

canoe to the star-scattered smaller ones, different groups of people came and settled. Some were dark-skinned and bushy-haired, some were brown-skinned, and some were tall, lightly tanned seafarers.

In the islands of Melanesia (*mel-uh-*NEE-*zhuh*)—those furthest west and closest to Asia—the people are darker. "Melanesia" comes from the Greek words meaning "black" and "island." The Fijis (FEE-*jeez*) are in this group. Micronesia (*my-kroh-*NEE-*zhuh*), which means the "small islands," lies to the north of Melanesia, and is made up of chains of tiny coral atolls that most people would never have heard of had they not played such a vital part in World War II. The Gilberts, the Marshalls, the Carolines and Marianas are still used as naval bases, airports and weather stations. Many of the Micronesians have Mongolian characteristics, and are similar to the Asiatic people who crossed over to Alaska and became the Eskimos and Indians of the Western Hemisphere.

Some time early in the Christian era, Polynesia (*pahl-ih-*NEE-*zhuh*)— "many islands"—was settled by the most remarkable people of all. These were the "Vikings of the Sunrise" who sailed eastward on the vast uncharted Pacific in their double canoes, and colonized the innumerable islands that include Samoa (*suh-*MOH-*uh*), Tonga, Tahiti (*tuh-*HE-*tee*), Hawaii and New Zealand. The Polynesians are as sunny and attractive as their islands, and their warmth and hospitality to strangers who have landed on their shores is legendary.

The driving force that thrust these peoples from their Asiatic homeland to venture with incredible courage over thousands of miles of ocean seems to have dwindled away today. Now they are easygoing, fun-loving, indolent, living contentedly from day to day like happy children on the bounty of their lovely islands. As a result, the men of more aggressive nations have taken over, and the South Pacific is largely under the paternal control of the United Kingdom, France, the United States and the Netherlands.

## FIJI, CROWN COLONY OF FORMER CANNIBALS

The Fiji Islands have an awesome past, for they were the renowned Cannibal Islands, where the natives' taste for "long pig"—their evasive name for human flesh—was finally discouraged just seventy years ago. In 1789, when Captain Bligh (*bly*) was cast adrift in an open boat by the mutineers of the *Bounty*, he and his companions steered a course through the Fijis, being careful not to land there. They were pursued by two canoes filled with fierce warriors, and even the intrepid Bligh admitted to "being apprehensive of their intentions." He reported in his journal, "we rowed with some Anxiety." Bligh charted a number of the 322 islands of the group, and for a while they were known officially by his name.

The bushy-haired Fijians fought voraciously among themselves for years, but their dietary habits discouraged Europeans from colonizing and bringing order to the fruitful islands. In the 1860s an island chief offered Fiji to the United States, but we were involved in the Civil War and did not reply. Finally, in spite of the frequent disappearance of missionaries into the stewpot, Queen Victoria accepted the Fiji Islands in 1874, and the British flag has flown over them ever since. The persistence of the missionaries and the firmness of British law eventually wiped out the last traces of cannibalism.

Today less than half the population is Fijian. These handsome, muscular giants, who were once renowned for their ferocity, are docile and happy-go-lucky now. Though they can sing and dance up a storm, their energy vanishes when there is work to be done. Consequently the British had to import East Indian laborers for the sugar plantations when they first took over the islands. By now the Indians far outnumber the Fijians, and what is more, they have monopolized commerce, agriculture and most of the more lucrative jobs on the islands. This has made for some friction between the two groups, but in a land where breadfruit grows on trees and the lagoons are filled with fish, life is too good to spoil with quarreling. Fiji is picturesque and colorful and deserves its sobriquet, "the jewel of the Commonwealth."

## TONGA, SMALLEST KINGDOM IN THE WORLD

About 80 miles to the east of Fiji the Pacific is peppered with a group of 200 tiny islands whose total area is only 259 square miles. This is the pleasant Kingdom of Tonga, ruled by the monumental and majestic Queen Salote (*sah-*LOH*-teh*). Her radiant smile won the hearts of the British when she attended Queen Elizabeth's coronation, and her striking personality put Tonga on the map then for millions of people who had never known of the only Polynesian kingdom in the Pacific. It is under the protection of Great Britain.

The name "Tonga" means south, and was probably given to these islands by their first settlers, the skillful Polynesian seafarers who migrated from Samoa, 500 miles to the northeast. The present Queen can trace her ancestry to chieftains who ruled here before the Norman Conquest of England. In the eighteenth century Captain James Cook, the British navigator who explored the South Pacific, made several voyages to Tonga. He found the natives so hospitable that he called their archipelago the Friendly Islands. It is a name that is still used, and in the gardens of the Queen's palace there is another relic of Cook's visit. An ancient tortoise, gift of the Captain to a Tongan chief, still crawls about, its torpid pace ideally suited to the timeless contentment of life on these islands.

Though time matters little to the natives of the South Seas, travelers have a perplexing experience with the calendar in this part of the world. The International Date Line cuts between some of the islands, and you find yourself losing a day when you go from east to west—from Samoa to Tonga or Fiji, for example. On the other hand you gain a day when traveling from west to east—a circumstance that Phileas Fogg forgot about in *Around the World in Eighty Days.* It gave him an extra twenty-four hours, enabling him to win his bet and get back to London within the prescribed time after all.

## SAMOA, POLYNESIAN PARADISE

Traveling from Tonga to Samoa you literally move back from today to yesterday. But the languid islands of Samoa, floating just 13 degrees south of the equator, are a return to South Seas yesterdays in another sense. Here was the cradle of Polynesian culture in the Pacific, and from Samoa hundreds of years ago the double canoes set forth to populate still other unknown islands. Today the Samoans are the purest remaining Polynesians, and their picturesque customs have been kept alive on these islands where the family and clan remain the important social and governing units.

The nine western islands were a United Nations Trust administered by New Zealand until 1962, when they became the first independent Polynesian state of this century. The six eastern islands are under the control of the United States Department of the Interior, but the Samoans themselves play a large part in their government.

The total area of American Samoa is only 76 square miles, and it was valuable to us chiefly because of the remarkable harbor at Pago Pago (PAN-*go* PAN-*go*). Once the crater of a huge volcano, the harbor is a great saucer of blue water surrounded on three sides by steep green hills. Until 1951 it was a U.S. Naval Station. Now it is a port of call for Pacific cruise ships whose passengers are eager to see tropical Pago Pago, scene of Somerset Maugham's famous story of Miss Sadie Thompson and the tormented missionary.

*Captain Bligh and eighteen men were forced to put to sea in a small boat by the Bounty mutineers.*

Western Samoa enjoys a literary fame of a different sort. Outside of Apia (*ah-*PEE-*ah*), its capital city, is the house where Robert Louis Stevenson spent his last years. Adored by the Samoans, who called him *Tusitala* (*too-see-*TAH-*lah*), the Teller of Tales, Stevenson is buried on a nearby mountaintop. The road that leads from Apia to his house was carved out of the jungle by his affectionate neighbors who named it the Road of the Loving Heart.

Not many tourists visit Western Samoa—an entry permit and a return ticket are required before an outsider can set foot on these paradisiacal islands. But once in Samoa, you will find that the happy Polynesians are courteous and gracious hosts. Their governments are wise to shield them from the outside world, for they have remained, as they were in Stevenson's time, "God's best, at least God's sweetest works."

## TAHITI, "PEARL OF THE PACIFIC"

The storied island of Tahiti was once a place of unspoiled innocence and beauty. When the first European explorers landed there in the eighteenth century, it was the perfect tropical dream island. With its green peaks rising from the sea, and the surf breaking in a white froth against the barrier reef that circles the island, Tahiti held the promise of an exotic heaven on earth. Captain Cook came to Tahiti in 1769 to observe the transit of Venus across the sun, and perhaps because of the earthly Venuses he found there he called it "Beloved Island."

The mutinous crew of the *Bounty,* after getting rid of tyrannical Captain Bligh, sailed back to Tahiti where they picked up their native sweethearts and then went on to found a new colony on Pitcairn Island. By this time Europe was beginning to hear such things about the fabulous South Sea island that a missionary group was sent from London to establish headquarters at Tahiti. Later, French missionaries came to the island of blue lagoons and waving palm trees in an attempt to counteract the influence of sailors on these carefree children of nature.

By 1880 Tahiti had become an official dependency of France and was part of French Polynesia—a colony that includes most of the islands of the southeast Pacific. Its main port, the capital city of Papeete (*pah-pay-*AY-*tay*), is a fascinating blend of France and Polynesia, and is known today as the Paris of the Pacific. The seductive lure of Tahiti is as strong as it ever was, but any dream that calls men over the seas is bound to disappoint them when they first see it in actuality. Papeete, the first taste of Tahiti, is no exception, and it has had its fair share of disillusioned criticism—it is honky-tonk, ramshackle, touristy, a tarnished and shopworn Eden.

"Where," the traveler asks himself after a long, tiring flight from his homeland, "where is the glorious, unspoiled Tahiti that Paul Gauguin painted?" At that moment it would be well to remember Gauguin's first impression of Tahiti. In 1891, after a sixty-three-day voyage from France, the painter who had abandoned his family and the civilized world for a South Seas dream found that "[Papeete] was Europe —the Europe which I had thought to shake off. . . . It was the Tahiti of former times which I loved. That of the present filled me with horror."

As everyone who has seen his paintings knows, Gauguin eventually found the bewitching Tahiti of his dreams. And furthermore, it still exists today. In the wild green depths of the island, on lonely coral beaches, beside sapphire lagoons framed by tall palm trees, we too can recapture that primeval world whose memory stirs in all of us, evoked by the magic of the South Seas.

*Mooréa, twelve miles from Tahiti, is as unspoiled as it was when Captain Cook sailed into this bay.*

let's travel in the

# SOUTH

# SEAS

# TROPICAL WATERFRONT: HARBOR AT PAPEETE

ALL the romance of the seven seas and the colorful ships that sail them seems to be crowded into the port of Papeete. Once this was a quiet harbor lying in the curve of a brilliant blue lagoon where natives paddled their outriggers. Those peaceful times are past, and if Papeete no longer has its pristine loveliness, it has instead the glamour and adventure that we associate with the fascinating craft that ply the South Pacific.

Here on Papeete's waterfront, ships from all over the world tie up right at the town's main street. Some days a great ocean liner rides at anchor, dwarfing the freighters, schooners, pearling luggers and graceful yachts lined up along the quay. The ever-present fragrance of tropical flowers is mixed with the sweet smell of vanilla and the heavy odor of copra (COPE-*ruh*)—dried coconut—as barefoot stevedores unload the cargo.

On boat days, when the large passenger vessels dock, the whole town turns out to greet them. Well, perhaps not the *whole* town—half of Tahiti's 30,000 inhabitants live in Papeete—but everyone who can turns up at the wharf with fresh flowers for the debarking tourists. As a first sight of this tropical island, to which many of the travelers have yearned to escape, it is rather overwhelming. Enthusiastic greeters swarm along the waterfront, and beyond the sea of milling people the streets are jammed with the regular procession of motor scooters, bicycles, taxis and automobiles that give this South Sea port the air of a busy metropolis.

The new arrivals head for their hotels as fast as they can, clinging fast to their dream of lazy beaches and a peaceful interlude under the palms.

16

# BLACK SAND BEACH: TAHITIAN PICNICKERS

THIS is the gay and carefree life that people picture when they think of Tahiti. And it is true that the golden-skinned islanders love laughter and good times and delight in living freely and joyously, on perpetual holiday. They let the sober, hard-working Chinese mind the shops while the French run the government. The Tahitians just live.

Their island was made for pleasure. Tahiti is shaped like a figure eight with two extinct volcanoes, one large and one small, forming the two circles of land. Around the margins of the figure eight are beaches and a strip of coastal land where tall palm trees sway. The lush growth includes trees bearing avocados, mangoes, breadfruit, bananas, low flat patches of taro, and on higher ground coffee shrubs and vanilla plants. There is a luxuriance of tropical flowers, and the Tahitians not only wear the fresh blossoms, but also use floral motifs in their distinctive cotton prints.

Inland, the wilderness takes over. The black volcanic rock, from which this velvet sand was made, rises in craggy peaks clothed in jungle green. Though the shores are bathed in sunshine, the mountains are veiled in mist and clouds, and they loom over the island, lonely and mysterious. The Tahitians seldom penetrate the rugged interior of their island. Why should they when they can picnic on beaches like this, with fruit to pick nearby and fish to catch in the clear blue-green water of the lagoon?

*"Le truck" is the Toonerville bus that makes its way around the coast road of Tahiti.*

# SOUTH SEA METROPOLIS: PAPEETE'S MAIN STREET

WHEN you tire of fishing in the lagoons or lazing on one of Tahiti's sunny beaches, there is always Papeete to come back to. Here we see the main street that runs along the waterfront, certainly the most picturesque section of this authentic South Sea port. The building facing us is the headquarters of the Donald Company, one of the largest trading concerns in the South Pacific. Its trading schooners, patched and sea-stained now, carry on the romantic tradition of tall-masted ships whose white sails were once familiar sights on the Pacific's horizon.

This crescent of waterfront is usually the busiest part of town, but we see it now in the daily lull that takes place between eleven and two o'clock. Shops close, business shuts down, the streets are all but deserted and for three hours the languorous Tahitian tempo replaces the hectic French pace of Papeete.

Fanning out from the waterfront with its shipping offices, small hotels, restaurants and bars, is a maze of narrow streets. Their wooden buildings are balconied and rather ramshackle, with tin roofs that soak up the tropical sun. The sidewalks are shaded by acacia and tamarind trees, and the steady stream of passers-by, babbling in French and Tahitian, give Papeete its distinctive character. Here you see the gorgeous island girls dressed in vivid prints, their blue-black hair falling to their waists, elegant Frenchwomen in smart Parisian clothes, Chinese gliding quietly by in their usual somber black, sporty yachtsmen, sailors out for a good time, and a sprinkling of tourists entranced at being part of this cosmopolitan scene.

# FRAGRANT GREETING: ISLAND HOSPITALITY

**T**HE friendly Polynesian custom of draping visitors with the flowers of the land is practiced in Tahiti as it is in Hawaii. When a passenger boat docks in Papeete, the townspeople celebrate the event by bringing armloads of flower garlands with which they welcome friends and strangers alike. There are also elderly flower ladies on hand who sell fragrant chains of blossoms—frangipani (*fran-jih-*PAN-*ih*), bright red hibiscus and the special flower of the island, *tiare* (*tee-*AH-*reh*) *Tahiti,* a small waxy gardenia whose perfume permeates the air.

Until recently Tahiti, for all its fame, had relatively few tourists. Nine hundred visitors a year was a lot, for the trip was long and difficult. But now a new jet airstrip has been built just a few miles outside of Papeete, and the hospitable Tahitians are getting ready to welcome 15,000 visitors this year! The little island may well become a second Hawaii, its remoteness dispelled by jet planes, its seductive languor transformed into summer-resort bedlam.

But for the present, Tahiti is still Tahiti. There is only one paved road that follows the seashore around the larger part of the island, connecting the scattered villages with Papeete. A rickety bus, known as "le truck," makes scheduled trips, picking up passengers, packages and lists of errands for the driver to perform in town, rather like the Toonerville Trolley. The countryside outside Papeete is ablaze with flamboyant flowers that glow against the lush greenery. Surely there will still be thousands blooming there even after garlands are woven for the many new arrivals.

# SULTRY BEAUTY: TRADEMARK OF TAHITI

SCOTLAND is famous for its tweeds, France for its wines, Switzerland is celebrated for fine watches, but Tahiti is renowned for its girls. The Polynesians were handsome people to begin with, and nearly two hundred years ago the first European voyagers to these islands were captivated by the grace and charm of the native beauties. Today the girls have a combination of Parisian chic and Polynesian dreaminess that is the very essence of Tahiti itself.

The *vahine* (*vah-HE-neh*) in this picture wears her garland and crown of tropical flowers as elegantly as if they were sable. The typical island dress is a length of gaily printed cotton called a *pareu* (*pah-REH-oo*). On Tahiti, where the missionary influence was less strong than on other islands, this sarong-like garment is apt to be fairly skimpy. But most of the young *vahines* are slim and graceful, and in this hot climate their brief attire is both sensible and attractive. In fact, after a few days in Tahiti, female tourists frequently head for the nearest Chinese dressmaker where they can have a *pareu* run up for a very small price. Tahiti's handsome people continue to be one of the island's chief attractions. You see them in colorful groups, laughing and gayly exchanging greetings as they gather around tables at one of Papeete's sidewalk cafes. Or, most memorably of all, you can watch them, flower-crowned and graceful, dancing their native dances.

*An island girl teaches a visitor how to go native.*

# HULA DRUMS:
# INVITATION
# TO THE
# DANCE

TO THE people of the South Seas, singing and dancing are as necessary as breathing. Their dances vary from island to island, and on Tahiti a particularly frenzied hula is the favorite. The Tahitians start young. Toddlers wear harmonicas around their necks and five-year-olds can strum a ukulele or beat a drum. By the time children are old enough to go to school they can perform a rhythmic hula as skillfully as their elders.

Stevedores unloading cargo from the ships sing and dance as they swing the heavy sacks ashore, turning their strenuous work into a ball. A picnic on the beach winds up with someone playing the ukulele so that everyone can dance, swaying more wildly than the palm trees. The hula is very good for the digestion, they will tell you.

When the heat of the day has been dispelled by the *hupe* (ноо-*peh*), a cool and fragrant night wind that blows from the mountains, the darkness throbs with hula drums. In the villages, under the fitful light of torches, teams of men and women dressed in grass skirts and adorned with flowers perform the dances of their ancestors. In the Hawaiian

*Bastille Day is celebrated for two mad weeks in French Tahiti, and these dancers show the strain.*

hula the story is told by the dancer's hands, but the Tahitian hula depends upon expressive hips that revolve and wriggle while the upper torso scarcely moves. As the drummers beat their wild rhythms the dancers gyrate, and their movements tell the oldest legends of their race.

# QUINN'S TAHITIAN HUT: TAVERN IN THE TROPICS

**P**ICTURESQUELY located on Papeete's waterfront, Quinn's is one of the liveliest, gaudiest cabarets in the South Seas. It is open all day for the convenience of thirsty sailors and beachcombers, who consume great quantities of beer, Tahiti's most popular drink. Although there are about half a dozen night clubs in Papeete, Quinn's is the number-one spot for both natives and tourists.

When the sun sets, a small orchestra blasts off near the bar, and then you begin to see why this little straw hut is world-famous. Tahitian girls and young men, many of them barefoot, get up and do their shack-shaking version of the hula. Those tourists who are not shocked into immobility at the sight frequently wriggle on to the dance floor, too, and East and West meet in a good-humored if not downright hilarious dance contest.

At 11:30 Papeete's night spots must shut up tight, but that does not mean the end of fun and laughter. Those who have them, clamber on their motor bikes, others drive or even walk out to the country where they resume dancing at the Lafayette, which is just opening at midnight. If they can't quite make it to the Lafayette, the merrymakers use the middle of the road for a dance floor.

The traditional end to Saturday night is reminiscent of Paris, where late celebrators wind up at the great outdoor market. Here in Papeete the dancers straggle back to town in time for the 5:00 A.M. opening of their market. As dawn begins to streak the tropical sky, the crowds mill around between mounds of fruit, vegetables and exotic fish, gossiping and haggling. The Chinese merchants, the townspeople and country folk are wide-awake. Only the Tahitian fishermen, who have been out all night catching their wares, and the revelers, who have been dancing since sundown, stumble home sleepily when the market closes.

# BY A BLUE LAGOON: LUXURY HOTEL

THE newer hotels in Tahiti ignore modern architecture and turn back instead to the old look of the island, when thatched huts stood beneath the palm trees. The primitive appearance of these little cottages is deceptive. They are actually the most luxurious accommodations to be had, equipped as they are with refrigerators, enormous baths, stall showers and that last word in tropical necessities—hot water.

The great tourist influx has created a shortage of hotel rooms on Tahiti, and so far few of the visitors have a desire to escape from civilization to the point of wanting to sleep under a palm tree. There are a number of small hotels in Papeete, but the most lavish ones are built along the lagoon outside of town. This makes them convenient to the new three-million-dollar airstrip that is just three and a half miles from the city.

Visitors who arrive by air have a less picturesque welcome than those who sail into the harbor of Papeete. In place of the throng of flower-bearing Tahitians, they are greeted by a fleet of French automobiles ready to whisk them off to their hotels. The life of a luxury beachcomber in one of these well-appointed thatched huts can be pretty expensive. Hotels charge as much as any metropolitan hotel without meals, and meals in Tahiti, where French foods are featured, can run high. Whatever happened to the simple life?

*Bicycles and motor scooters are the chief vehicles on the streets of Papeete.*

# HUSKY ISLANDER: THE HAPPY LIFE

LIFE is still simple for this husky fellow, sitting on a pile of copra sacks. Fat and good natured, he is typical of the Polynesians who grow heavy and flabby in their middle years as a result of easy living. The lithe and agile young people, whose good looks add so much to the islands' beauty, all must come to this some day.

One of the local characters is a mountain of a man in his sixties who is a living reminder of one of the most famous South Sea idyls. He is the son of the French painter Paul Gauguin and Tehura (*teh-HOO-rah*), the Polynesian girl whom the artist loved. Gauguin wrote of his years in Tahiti, "Happiness and work rose up together with the sun, radiant like it. The gold of Tehura's face flooded the interior of our hut and the landscape round about with joy and light."

Gauguin died in the South Seas about sixty years ago, leaving the world a legacy of sun-splashed paintings that capture the innocence and dazzling beauty of the islands. After his death there was an auction in Papeete of the artist's possessions. His dishes, his coffeepot and household utensils brought more money than the paintings found in the house. Most of his works were bought for a few francs each by a couple of French naval lieutenants who were amateur artists. Evidently they did not share the opinion, current in Papeete at the time, that Gauguin was a crackpot because he painted people with purple hair and lemon yellow faces.

# TROPICAL WILDERNESS: THE LAST PARADISE

**T**HIS is the Tahiti that Gauguin delighted to paint, lush and primitive, inhabited by a sunny and gentle people. This is the South Sea dream shared by many of us, of a world that is still fresh and young and bountiful. And when we really see it at last, we are thankful that there are places on this island that have not yet been changed by civilization.

And how do these people live in their hidden paradise? They have not known war for over a hundred years. They are strangers to cold, to floods, to famine and to many of the diseases that our cosmopolitan flesh is heir to. In the remote sections of Tahiti and on the neighboring island of Mooréa (*moh-oh-*RAY*-uh*)—the Bali Ha'i of Michener's *South Pacific*—life is reduced to a carefree simplicity.

A man has a little land, and in its rich soil brilliant flowers and trees, heavy with fruit, grow without help from him. The ocean gives him fish. The coral reef beyond the lagoon supplies him with clams and lobsters, the river that courses down from the green hills carries delicious little fresh-water shrimp. The tall, slim palm trees bear coconuts, and though money doesn't grow on trees—even in paradise—the coconuts can be readily converted into cash.

All a man has to do is wait for the nuts to fall to the ground. Then he cracks them open with an ax, and in a few days he can remove the meat from the shell. The meat dries in the sun for about twelve days, and must be covered at night and turned with a pitchfork once each day. At the end of that time the man has—copra. It is good for seven cents a pound at the general store, where he can purchase pots and pans, hardware, cloth or kerosene when he needs it. While the Chinese shopkeeper is busy with his bookkeeping and inventory and occupied with his eternal buying and selling, our man goes free, out into the world with flowers in his hair and the endless lovely hours to spend with his family and friends.

# TAHITIAN CHURCH: WORK OF THE MISSIONARIES

ALTHOUGH missionaries came to Tahiti as early as 1797, and there are a number of small churches on the island, religion is taken lightly by these carefree people. Eighteen Methodist clergymen who sailed from London were the first to try to Christianize the Polynesians. They imposed a strict and intolerant rule over the people, working through the Tahitian kings of the Pomare (*poh*-MAH-*reh*) dynasty.

The missionaries set up a printing press and planted sugar, cotton and coffee. King Pomare II renounced heathenism, and a number of his subjects became Christian converts, too. But there was a general backsliding some years later when King Pomare II died. In 1836 Catholic priests from France tried to open a mission in Tahiti, but Queen Pomare, backed by the English missionaries, refused to allow them to stay. The French sent a frigate to Tahiti and put the island under their protection. In 1880 King Pomare V formally handed his kingdom over to France, and it has been a French colony ever since, with complete religious freedom.

There are Protestant and Catholic churches on the island today, and if you drive along Tahiti's one road on a Sunday you will pass a number of these wayside churches. From each of them the sound of hymn-singing comes pouring out as the musical Polynesians perform their favorite part of the services with gusto.

*An altar painting shows a religious scene with landscape and figures that are Tahitian.*

37

# OLD STONE
# TIKI:
# PAGAN
# IDOL

THE ancient religion of the Polynesians has languished, existing today only in ruined temples and relics like this one, and in superstitions that crop up unexpectedly. Although the majority of Tahitians are at least nominal Christians, the old taboos still have significance for them. For instance, this tiki (TEE-*kee*) stood guard at the entrance of a museum in Tahiti, and when the museum was moved none of the workmen dared to touch the sacred image. So it was abandoned to stare solemnly over the lush plants that are encroaching on its domain.

The idol in this picture is seven feet high and it was carved about five hundred years ago. In the old days tikis protected the outdoor temples, or maraés (*mah*-RAH-*ayz*), that were built deep in the lonely green valleys. The wind that whistled through the trees was called "the voice of the gods," and Tahitian priests used to come at night to listen to the sounds in the sacred groves and interpret their messages to the people.

*The tomb of the last Tahitian king, Pomare V, is topped symbolically with a giant bottle.*

The maraés were enclosures built of lava and coral, with a broad altar where offerings of fish and bananas were made to the gods. Sometimes there were human sacrifices, but they were placed on the altar carefully covered, and were euphemistically known as "Long Fish." It is not surprising that a tiki, embodiment of an old god brooding in the green silence, can still strike awe into the hearts of the islanders.

38

# TIKI CARVER: ISLAND OF MOOREA

TAHITIAN craftsmen continue to carve grotesque tikis, though the images are no longer used to guard their temples. There is a brisk tourist business in these exotic souvenirs and you can have one made to order and shipped anywhere you wish. Shopping in Papeete is a fascinating experience, for it is a French port, which means that perfumes, crystal, Parisian costume jewelry, and other products of France can be found in the middle of the South Pacific. Since most of the shops are Chinese, they reflect their owners' enterprising ability to collect odds and ends from all over this part of the world. Carved shell bric-a-brac, pearls brought in by native divers, hula skirts from Bora Bora, and objects made of bamboo, wood or straw crowd the shelves of dingy Chinese stores.

The man in our picture is working far from the bustle of Papeete. The island of Mooréa is only twelve miles from Tahiti but it is another world. The Bali Ha'i of *South Pacific* was inspired by Mooréa whose dramatic peaks are sometimes completely hidden behind great banks of cloud. At other times the clouds lift and the island reappears on the horizon as if by magic. A three-hour launch trip over rough water brings you to the spectacular little bay of rustic Mooréa. Here, within sight of Papeete, is the seclusion, remoteness and unspoiled beauty of long-ago Polynesia.

A narrow dirt road circles the island, and there are fewer than fifty cars on Mooréa. There is a good hotel on the island, but since it can accommodate only twenty guests there is not much danger of Mooréa's being ruined by crowds of people eager to escape from other crowds of people. Only when a cruise ship is docked in Papeete do tourists in any number flock to Mooréa. On those occasions a *tamaaraa* (tah-mah-ah-RAH-*ah*), or native feast, is prepared, and afterwards a dance group from one of the villages stages a lavish hula spectacle by torchlight.

# CHILDREN OF NATURE: WATER BABIES

IF LIFE on these islands is a delight for adults, it is even more wonderful for children. There are schools for them, of course, but with summertime enjoyments to be had 365 days a year the classroom routine is uniquely Tahitian. Those parts of the day devoted to fishing and swimming benefit the children as much as the more academic subjects because they will be a major part of their adult daily life.

The Tahitians do not sport around in the open ocean as the Hawaiians do. Though they, too, have inherited a love of aquatic activities from their Polynesian ancestors, they prefer to swim in the fresh water of their green rivers. Evidently the Tahitians believe that salt-water swimming is unhealthy. And in this part of the world they may have a point.

Their Eden has no serpents or snakes, but in the clear blue waters of the lagoons the dread stonefish lives. This lethal creature is about a foot long and it lurks in the coral formations where the water is shallow. It is so adept at camouflage that people frequently step on a stonefish thinking it is part of the rock. Poison from the spines on the fish's back immediately starts its deadly work, and unless an antidote is administered quickly, the victim may be bedridden and in agony for a month, or may even die.

Rats and land crabs do their bit to keep this from being a perfect paradise. If you look closely at the tall palm trees in this lovely grove you will see that each one has a wide metal band encircling its trunk. The slippery surface prevents rodents from reaching the upper fronds where the coconuts grow. But in spite of any drawbacks, existence in Tahiti is joyous. The laughing faces of these children are living proof.

# FLOWER WOMEN: JOLLY MATRONS

**T**HE slim golden girls of Tahiti age quickly in the tropics, but though they may lose their youth and their looks they keep their happy dispositions. With age comes enormous girth and an equally enormous zest for life. These fat Tahitian women are the most colorful characters on the island, and you can see them selling flowers with enthusiasm or bossing the crews of fishing boats and small interisland vessels at the dock. They waste no time in regrets for the past, because from childhood on they have crammed each day with pleasure. The Tahitian philosophy of "never mind" makes their lives as sunny as their climate.

There are no newspapers in Tahiti, but rumor and gossip travel with incredible speed, thanks to talkative Polynesians like these flower sellers. They have a passionate interest in everything that is going on, and their loud, cheery voices spread the information up and down the waterfront where it is picked up by crews of ships that will be sailing to other islands. To Europeans and Americans, who are accustomed to mechanized channels of communication, it seems miraculous that the "coconut radio" can be so effective. There are more than 10,000 isolated islands in the South Pacific, yet their inhabitants seem to know all about one another. These good-natured gossips can reduce the whole vast South Pacific to the status of a small town.

*The "coconut radio," as island gossip is called, broadcasts whenever ladies meet.*

# FLAG DAY: AMERICAN SAMOA

ABOUT 1200 miles to the west of Tahiti are the tiny islands of American Samoa, her only outpost in the South Pacific. The Stars and Stripes have been flying over them since 1900, and here, against a background of tropical green, we see part of the gala Flag Day celebration. Every April 17 the islanders stage a Samoan spectacular to commemorate the ceding of their islands to the United States. On that date Samoan chiefs voluntarily signed an Instrument of Cession with President William McKinley, who then gave each an inscribed silver watch.

Originally the U. S. Navy used the fine harbor of Pago Pago as a coaling station, and during World War II the islands were a strategic base. Now they are under the jurisdiction of the Department of Interior, and the Navy has pulled out, leaving a large gap in the islands' economy. But

*When the Navy governed here Samoan M.P.s, known as Fita-Fitas, wore these unusual uniforms.*

tourist gold may soon fill that gap when the new jet airstrip is completed. Up until now the islands of Samoa, with their thickly forested mountains and scenic beaches, have had little contact with the outside world. The people have been encouraged to retain their traditional Samoan way of life, but there are indications that they have outgrown that archaic and undemocratic system. Though the men still wear the wrap-around lava-lavas, they have learned English in school and are well aware of the political ideals of Washington, Jefferson and Lincoln.

# HIGH CHIEF: VILLAGE HEADMAN

**T**HE old Samoan social system that has endured for hundreds of years is based upon family groups under the leadership of a village chief, called a *matai* (*mah*-TAH-*ee*). His powers are absolute, and he assigns occupations to each member of his clan, divides earnings among all and holds the family lands in trust. In the Western world, power tends to corrupt, but among the easygoing Samoans it simply gives the chief an added dignity and strength.

The high chief is frequently a man of imposing physique, for among the Polynesians size and girth are attributes of authority. The chief wears a lava-lava usually bound at the waist with a wide girdle of tapa cloth. A ceremonial necklace of shells hangs on his bare chest. This august personage does not communicate directly with his people on matters of state. Instead he has an intermediary known as a talking chief. Samoan talking chiefs are famed for their flowery and long-winded oratory which they have developed to a degree that would make any politician envious. They can be hired by anyone to deliver birthday greetings or speeches for any occasion.

The government of American Samoa depends to a large extent upon the village chiefs. The top administrator is a governor appointed by the President of the United States, but under him there are three district governors chosen from the ranks of county chiefs. Below them is the hierarchy of county and village headmen, local leaders like the man in our picture, whose word on community affairs is final. The legislature has 66 members of which 64 must be natives. James Michener, author of *Tales of the South Pacific*, says of these people, "The men and women walk like gods with unmatched dignity. Never will you see in London or Paris old men so handsome as these Samoans. They are politically alert and intellectually able."

# STREET
# IN APIA:
# CAPITAL OF
# WESTERN SAMOA

YOU can fly from American Samoa to Western Samoa in forty-five minutes, landing on the main island of Upolu (*oo*-POH-*loo*) where Apia is situated on a curving bay. The two Samoas are much alike, but in these islands, which used to be administered by New Zealand, you will notice that the village children play cricket rather than baseball, which is the favorite game on the sandlots of Pago Pago.

The missionary influence is strong throughout Samoa. You see it particularly in the modest garb of the women, who wear their lava-lavas down to their ankles and for good measure put a cotton dress over them. It is also apparent in the numerous churches—there are at least twelve in Apia alone. Samoans attend several services each Sunday where their strong voices are raised in a spirited rendition of the hymns.

Samoa, unlike many of the other South Pacific islands, has had little infiltration of other peoples. The population is predominantly Samoan—the tall, handsome, full-blooded Polynesian type at its best. Furthermore the birth rate is climbing so rapidly (more than half the people are under eighteen years of age) that the Samoans find it necessary to keep their beautiful country for themselves. Their agricultural economy presents greater problems than running their own government.

The climate here is less overwhelmingly tropical than in Tahiti. The luxuriance of growing things is more restrained, and the heat is bearable. Nevertheless, a popular place in Apia is "the Coolest Spot in Town" building, which we see here. It looks like an old-time saloon, but since there are no bars in Apia, the Coolest Spot is patronized for its ice-cream refreshments.

# THATCHED HOUSE: SKILLFUL ARCHITECTURE

THERE are nearly two hundred villages on the island of Upolu dotted along the shoreline. Large or small they are all composed with an artist's eye for pleasing effect, with the houses seeming to grow as a natural part of the landscape. The Samoans are considered to be the finest architects of the Pacific, and their houses, called *fales* (FAH-*less*), are unique and picturesque. The *fale* is built like a pavilion, with posts of palm or breadfruit trunks spaced at regular intervals around a raised circular floor of dark volcanic stones. A shaggy, domed roof of thatch tops off the summerhouse, which has neither windows nor doors.

Blinds of coconut fronds can be lowered in case of a storm, but the Samoans wouldn't dream of using the blinds for privacy. They live their lives right out in the open, though the large interior of the house can be divided into sections with pieces of cloth stretched from a central pole to one of the posts. A Samoan house contains little furniture—perhaps a table or two and, in a chief's Long House, such refinements as a radio or sewing machine. Woven straw mats cover the floor and it is there that the Samoans eat and sleep.

For ceremonial feasts the guests sit cross-legged in a circle. It is very bad form to stretch your legs out in front of you with your feet pointed toward someone else. Though the Samoans are fun-loving and merry, they have great dignity and pride, and a careful etiquette governs their relationships with one another.

*A Samoan house is open to the breeze, and has little privacy.*

53

# DISTRICT HOSPITAL: GOVERNMENT HEALTH SERVICE

IN 1962 the people of Western Samoa became completely self-governing. The villages continued their communal way of life under the leadership of a chief, or *matai*, with the central government handling the problems of health, education and sanitation. There are no doctors in private practice, and hospitals and pharmacies are government-operated. Fortunately the Samoans are not plagued by many of the more terrible tropical diseases, although yaws, hookworm and tuberculosis are fairly prevalent, as they are in most of the South Sea islands.

The government hospital at Apia is the largest, but there are smaller ones like this scattered through the country. Evidently modern methods cannot improve upon the Samoan style of house, even for a hospital. The domed roof of thatch and open sides are admirably suited to the climate, the materials are cheap, and a patient in this kind of hospital is far from being a shut-in. Furthermore the nurses can't disappear out of sight at the end of a corridor when they get together to gab and compare notes. They are in full view of their patients, who have only to holler across the yard if they want attention. Free medical and dental care is given to Samoan children, and doctors visit the outlying districts on regular tours. Little by little, progress is being made to improve the health standards of these idyllic islands.

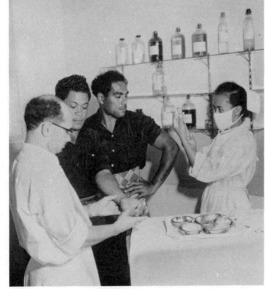

*Throughout the South Pacific, islanders are being trained for medical work.*

# KINGDOM OF TONGA: ROYAL FAMILY

ONE of the most remarkable island groups in the South Pacific is Tonga. Through its long history, it has never been controlled by a foreign power, and though the Tongans signed a treaty of friendship with Great Britain, they are ruled by their own royal family. Queen Elizabeth II of England and Queen Salote of Tonga are the only royal rulers in the Commonwealth.

In this picture we see one of Salote's two sons. The Queen has been widowed for many years, and the two Princes, both young and heroically proportioned, hold important posts in the government. The Prince is wearing the Tongan national dress—a high-necked tunic, a wraparound skirt called a *vala* (VAH-*lah*), and the broad straw mat around his waist known as the *ta'ovala* (*tah-oh-*VAH-*lah*). The straw mat symbolizes humility and modesty, and its size and quality vary according to the occasion. For funerals a coarse, roughly woven, tattered *ta'ovala* would be worn. An important ceremony would merit the finest and oldest mat one possessed. The Queen sometimes wears a precious heirloom over five hundred years old, as delicately woven as linen.

When Salote (whose name is the Tongan version of Charlotte) went to London for Queen Elizabeth's coronation, she rode in an open coach in spite of a pouring rain. She was paying tribute to the English Queen in the Tongan manner. Her subjects, as a mark of extreme respect to her, wait for a good rainstorm to blow up. Then they walk past the royal palace with umbrellas furled. They are wet, their Queen is dry; this is the ultimate in gracious compliments. The royal palace, situated on the bay, is a gabled white frame house decorated with Victorian jigsaw curlicues. On one of its porches, kava (KAH-*vah*), the Tongan ceremonial drink, is almost continuously being served to visiting notables. There is a dignity and pride about the Tongans, yet at the same time a small-town informality pervades their little kingdom.

# PACKING BANANAS: TONGA'S CHIEF EXPORT

THE capital of the Friendly Islands is a sleepy little town called Nukualofa (*noo-koo-ah*-LAW-*fah*), or Love's Place. It is the seat of the Tongan government and also the chief port of the islands. On the large palace lawn the citizens of Nukualofa meet as on a village green. The town gossip is exchanged, couples walk dreamily, arm in arm, in the fresh trade breeze, and in the afternoon British-style football or cricket is the big attraction.

But once or twice a month the banana boat from New Zealand puts in at Nukualofa. Tonga sells about 160,000 cases of the fruit to New Zealand each year, and it is the largest export crop of this agricultural country. So Steamer Day in Tonga takes on all the trappings of a national holiday. Then the palace lawn is reserved for the packing of banana crates which, in this tropical climate, is accomplished at an unhurried tempo and in the shade. There are frequent pauses for refreshment, and what with the townspeople celebrating the gala event, and the unusual activity on the lawn, Steamer Day resembles a big, happy picnic.

The Tongans were converted to Christianity in the nineteenth century by Wesleyan missionaries, and though full freedom of worship is permitted now, the laws reflect a strict Methodism. All work is forbidden on Sunday, as is any form of play. Fishing or golf are firmly prohibited on the Sabbath, even for foreigners living in Tonga. (There are fewer than three hundred Europeans there now.) So severe is the missionary attitude toward nakedness that a male Tongan over six years of age who appears in public stripped to the waist is subject to a heavy fine. Even the banana packers, working throughout the hot day to ready their cargo for the waiting ship, must keep their shirts on. These men, in spite of their Polynesian heritage, would undoubtedly be shocked at the sight of an American beach.

# BUILDING
# A HOUSE:
# COMMUNITY
# PROJECT

TONGA is a happy kingdom whose 58,000 souls enjoy the benefits of a well-run government. There is no national debt, and income tax is negligible. For years the people have benefited from a free health service and free compulsory education. Their Polynesian regard for family and clan has made orphanages or old peoples' homes unnecessary. And the Tongan land system is unique. All land is the property of the Crown, but none of it may be bought or sold. At the age of sixteen every young man receives an allotment of eight-and-a-quarter acres of farm land and a town site large enough to build a house on. He pays about $4.50 a year for taxes and must comply with certain planting laws in order to maintain a life interest in the land. The system seems to work remarkably well.

The Tongan government is also concerned about housing, and it insists that no house may be less than twelve feet long. Actually the average Tongan builds himself a home that is twenty feet long and twelve feet wide. Villages composed of airy palm huts with thatched roofs are beautiful and sensible in this climate. But the Tongans, perhaps in a misguided desire to modernize, have built a great number of European-style houses —stuffy wooden boxes with corrugated tin roofs. Fortunately, these building materials have been hard to get lately, and there has been a return to the native architecture we see here, graceful and true to old island tradition.

*Queen Salote entertained Queen Elizabeth and the Duke of Edinburgh when they visited Tonga in 1953.*

# FIJIAN FAMILY: DESCENDANTS OF CANNIBALS

THE Fiji Islands, only 80 miles northwest of Tonga, are on the dividing line between the dark-skinned Melanesians and the lighter Polynesians of the Pacific. Polynesians from Tonga were able to sail on the westerly trade winds to Fiji, and a number of them made the voyage long before the Europeans came. They traveled to Fiji in order to obtain the hard timber and know-how for building the big war canoes that were a Fijian specialty. Since it took seven years to build one, the visiting Tongans had ample time in which to influence their neighbors, and we can see that influence in the shape of this Fijian house.

These houses, called *vales* (VAH-*lehs*), have a steep roof of thatch, square-ended and hanging from a ridgepole of dark coconut log. The sides of the *vale* are thatched too, giving the house the same shaggy look as the famous Fijian headdress. These are an intelligent, proud and clever people, though they used to be brutal, dangerous, and confirmed in their cannibalistic practices. The remarkable task of gentling the savage Fijians was performed within one century by zealous—and courageous—missionaries. They brought Christianity and education to a people who were at first reluctant to accept them. Today the Fijians are fun-loving and peaceful, and their fearsome cannibal drums have been moved into the churches where their booming is a summons to worship instead of to feast.

*A special comb is used to achieve the outstanding Fijian headdress.*

# GOVERNOR'S GUARD: CEREMONY IN SUVA

**M**ORE than half the total area of Fiji is contained in Viti Levu (VEE-*tee* LEH-*voo*), the capital island whose name means Great Fiji. Here, at the hub of the South Pacific where sea and air routes converge, is Suva (soo-*vuh*), Fiji's capital city. With a population of almost 40,000 people, Suva is second only to Honolulu as an important Pacific city. But where Honolulu is an American metropolis, the accent in Suva is British.

These well-drilled Fijian guards in their colorful uniforms reflect the spit and polish that has always accompanied British colonial rule. In 1874 Fiji became a Crown Colony, and the British set about bringing order out of the chaotic tribal wars. As James Michener has written, "The British could easily have governed a bunch of savage islands from mean shacks. But if you believed that one day all the world would know order, you built stately and pillared mansions, even at the edge of the jungle. To do so gave an earnest of your intentions."

In Suva a broad green lawn, a spacious sports field and flower gardens are spread out near the bay as a setting for imposing government buildings. Fiji has a British governor, but its Legislative Council is composed of European, Indian and Fijian members. The war club of the last cannibal king, Thakombau (*thah-kohm*-BOW), is now the Council's mace. Thakombau gave the massive weapon to Queen Victoria when he ceded his country to her. He had it ornamented with silver leaves and sent it to his new monarch with a graceful pledge that indicated the remarkable changes wrought by the missionaries. "The King gives Her Majesty his old and favorite war club, the former and, until lately, the only known law of Fiji. In abandoning club law and adopting the forms and principles of civilized societies, he laid by his old weapon and covered it with the emblems of peace. . . ."

# MODERN
# LABOR LEADER:
# NATIONAL
# HEADDRESS

**T**HE Fijians are tall and muscular, and many of them, both men and women, top off their magnificent physiques with a shock of frizzy hair. A wooden comb the size and shape of a pancake turner is used to fluff out the coiffure so that it stands away as much as six inches from the scalp. This distinctive style is a source of great pride to the Fijians, and they consider it a serious social offense to touch a person's head. At one time such a display of rudeness was punishable by death.

The missionaries disapproved of the wild and woolly hair, and having taught the Fijians to clothe their nakedness, they then attempted to introduce them to Western barbering. Many of the male "big heads" saw military service in the last war, and they had to crop their proud manes in order to fit into their helmets. But today a great number of Fijians wear the national headdress with dignity, as a badge of their origin.

When the British took over in Fiji they imported thousands of Indians to work the sugar and copra plantations. The Indians have thrived to the point where they now outnumber the Fijians. They have demanded a voice in the government and ownership of land which has always belonged to Fijians, and as a consequence there are stirrings of nationalism in the islands. "Fiji for the Fijians" may soon be the rallying cry of these good-natured people who have, until now, been delighted to leave the hard work of their islands to alien laborers. Increased political sophistication has resulted in the growth of trade unions, and the labor leader in this picture is typical of the modern Fijian who is playing an increasingly important role in his country's affairs. A few have been educated at Oxford, but they remain a blend of the two cultures. Although shirt, jacket and tie may come from Bond Street in London, these men still wear the traditional *sulu*, a skirt-like garment, and many further proclaim their nationality by the cut of their hair.

# ANCIENT WAR DANCE: TERRIFYING SPECTACLE

**L**EST anyone forget that the charming well-mannered Fijians of the twentieth century have a heritage of brutality, they have kept alive the fierce old dances. The *meke* (MEH-*keh*) is a combination of rhythmical chant, the beating of a *lali* (LAH-*lee*), or ceremonial drum, and a group dance. In this spear *meke* the muscular men are dressed in kilts of long grass, and they hold palm-leaf shields in one hand while brandishing dangerous-looking spears in the other.

A group of men and women sitting on the ground chant and clap their hands to give the dancers the beat. The words of their song tell of past deeds, for they are the only historical records the Melanesians have. Lately, as the warriors go through their intricate drill, stamping their enormous feet and threatening with their spears, the lyrics have been concerned with more modern events. Fijian battalions performed in the last war with unmatched valor. In the Solomons and New Guinea these incomparable jungle fighters distinguished themselves, their ancestral skills and cunning emerging when they were most needed. The World War II battles, for which many Fiji soldiers won high decorations, are sometimes described in the setting of a ceremonial *meke*, but the spectacle is more likely to conjure up thoughts of headhunters rather than heroes.

*Fijian fire walkers step barefoot on white-hot rocks without burning their feet.*

# TRAFFIC
# POLICEMAN:
# SUVA'S
# FINEST

IN A LIST of "Tips for the Tourist" compiled by the Fiji Visitors Bureau, there are two points illustrated by this picture: "Always wear a hat as the sun is stronger than you think," and "Don't forget your camera as Fiji is a photographer's paradise." Though the inhabitants of Suva seem to be able to stand the tropical sun beating down on their uncovered heads, the traffic officers are given brightly colored umbrellas to protect them from the fierce rays. Fijian police are a colorful sight in their white *sulus* zigzagged at the bottom, possibly as a carry-over from the leaf skirts worn by their ancestors.

This policeman, directing traffic on one of Suva's downtown streets, is a fascinating subject for tourist photography. He is conveniently located in front of one of the numerous camera supply stores in Suva, for it is true that picture-taking is an irresistible activity for most visitors to Fiji. The capital city is exotic and cosmopolitan, a place of contrasts with a special South Pacific flavor. Backed by brilliant green hills and facing a harbor sheltered by coral reefs, Suva is a city of large modern buildings, broad thoroughfares and narrow, winding streets. On its

*This picturesque little train is operated by a sugar company which lets passengers ride free.*

sidewalks you will see tall Fijians in *sulus*, delicate Indian women wrapped in saris, Chinese, and natives from distant South Sea islands, as well as Europeans. And the shops, most of them run by Chinese and Indians, are like dark caves filled with the treasures and the oddities of far places.

# INDIAN SHOPKEEPER: FIJI'S MERCHANT CLASS

IN SUVA, turbaned Sikhs (SEEKS) and Hindus in flowing robes make up the majority of the population. Brought from their overcrowded homeland in the last century to work on the sugar plantations for the British, these people, by their industry and stamina, made Fiji the wealthiest Crown Colony in the Pacific. They are still called "sugar Indians," but today that is an inaccurate term, as their diligence has carried them beyond the sugar fields until now they are the backbone of the islands' commerce. They are traders, craftsmen and shopkeepers, and transact about 90 per cent of Fiji's banking business, as well as being the chief sugar-growers of the islands.

The range of the Indians' shops is enormous. Go to the city markets and you will see women like this one presiding over a variety of fruits and vegetables—some familiar, others you have never seen or heard of before. Other merchants have little cubbyholes filled with Indian handicrafts—filigreed silver, tortoise shell, sari cloth. There are shops where Indian tailors sit cross-legged on the floor, working at fantastic speed to make dresses, shirts or suits to order, quickly enough to satisfy the most impatient customer. And the Indian traders traffic in curios from the Orient and Fijian products such as kava bowls, tapa cloth and war clubs that were never designed to be crammed into suitcases.

The native Fijian, while he might work in his own village as an artisan, would never bother to get involved in the marketing of his wares. The fertile land belongs to him by immemorial right, and the British promised to protect his claims when they took over the islands. So the Fijian doesn't have to worry about getting enough to eat. His land supports him. Looking around at the Indians and Europeans who work so hard to make enough money to retire, the Fijian grins happily. He was born retired.

# LITTLE STRAW
# SCHOOLHOUSE:
# ENGLISH
# LESSON

THERE is just one way a Fijian child can avoid going to school. If he lives more than three miles from the nearest classroom he may play hooky. Otherwise, from the ages of six to fourteen, he is expected to sit at a desk and learn things that his people didn't even dream of a century ago. We must remember that when the first Europeans came here, the Fijians were still living in the primitive stone age. Their weapons, canoes, house timbers and utensils were made—and beautifully made—with only tools of stone. Their social practices were correspondingly primitive. Naturally, they had no written language.

When the Methodist missionaries arrived in 1835 they established schools and a training center and set about putting the Fijian language into writing. Now there are more than five hundred schools in Fiji, but the problems of reaching all the potential pupils are enormous. The 106 inhabited islands of the group are scattered over 10,000 square miles of the Pacific, and sometimes it takes months for administrative forms to get from Suva to one of the more remote schools. This may be a blessing in disguise, as it leaves the schoolmaster more time to teach because official paper work is kept to a minimum.

Then there is the problem of teaching children who speak a variety of Fijian dialects and children who speak various Indian languages. English is taught from first grade on in all schools, but there are separate establishments for Indian and Fijian children. In this picture we see a classroom in a rural Fijian school. The building is made of woven pandanus leaves and is an example of the islanders' skillful native craftsmanship. A picture of Queen Elizabeth, who visited Fiji in 1953, smiles down on her young subjects as they struggle with the intricacies of the English language. "Mutual Conversation" is the lesson for the day, and these boys are learning to speak politely to one another—a very different approach from that of their warlike ancestors.

# DANCE FESTIVAL: SCHOOLGIRL PERFORMANCE

FIJIAN women were not educated beyond the primary grades until fairly recently, but now there are intermediate and secondary schools for girls, and women are even entering the Civil Service and the medical profession. The old songs and dances are so vital a part of Fijian culture that they are retained in the schools as an inspiring addition to the three R's. These young students are gravely performing one of the traditional *mekes* in which they chant, clap their hands and stamp rhythmically. Except for their Melanesian faces they might be figures on an ancient Greek vase executing an old Mediterranean dance.

"Music hath charms to soothe the savage breast," and it was through the Fijians' love of music that the missionaries first won them to Christianity. There are no more ardent hymn-singers in the whole South Pacific, and that is saying a great deal. In the Anglican Church in Suva the organ has certain keys that create the authentic booming of cannibal drums, a sound that now accompanies the fervent chanting of religious songs. To satisfy the Fijians' desire to dance, the missionaries invented the *tralala*, a harmless shuffle in which dancers stand side by side—*never* face to face—and shamble around the dirt floor. Not very exciting, perhaps, but since an authentic *tralala* must last until sunup, it is guaranteed to give everyone more than enough dancing.

*Young Fijians are taught to use the weapons of modern civilization.*

77

# SOUTH SEA VISION: PACIFIC SUNSET

FEW people who come to the South Seas remain there. Like every dream, this one must end with an awakening, a return to brisker countries from these languorous islands. The evening sky beyond Papeete is flecked with clouds that wander from one island to another, blown by the trade winds. They are called *raireva* (*rye*-REH-*vah*), the Restless Ones, and the Polynesians have given that name to the strangers who visit their islands briefly, then move on.

We have imposed a new and complex civilization on the people of the South Pacific and in searching for our Paradise we have irretrievably altered theirs. But the splendor of a tropical sunset remains unchanged, and it casts a glow of mystery and beauty over a workaday scene such as this one. A freighter riding at anchor while a file of stevedores unloads her cargo becomes a symbol of romance when we see it against the backdrop of the South Seas. These tiny islands in the vast Pacific give us a vision of a different world, lovely in its simplicity, changeless in spite of change. In their elemental wisdom the islanders understand the secret of their world when they say, "The coral spreads, the palm trees grow . . . and only man departs."

*Islanders have learned to say farewell gracefully when the white ships sail away.*

78

# SOME FAMOUS NAMES IN SOUTH SEAS HISTORY

ABEL JANSZOON TASMAN (c. 1603-1659)—*Dutch navigator and discoverer of Tasmania, New Zealand, Tonga and the Fiji Islands.*

JAMES COOK (1728-1779)—*English explorer who led numerous expeditions throughout the South Pacific area. He charted the coasts of New Zealand, Australia, and New Guinea. On one of his many voyages he observed the transit of Venus in Tahiti.*

LOUIS ANTOINE DE BOUGAINVILLE (1729-1811)—*French navigator, who commanded first French expedition around the world (1766-69). Tropical flowering vine Bougainvillaea is named for him.*

WILLIAM BLIGH (1754-1817)—*English naval officer; captain of H.M.S. Bounty at the time of the famous mutiny.*

POMARE I (Eighteenth Century)—*In 1797 Chief Arii Rahii of Tahiti took the name Pomare and established the ruling dynasty by that name.*

POMARE V (Nineteenth Century)—*Tahitian ruler who ceded Tahiti to France in 1880.*

THAKOMBAU (Nineteenth Century)—*Fijian king who ceded Fiji to Great Britain in 1874.*

GEORGE TUBOU I (Nineteenth Century)—*Tongan chief Taufaahau assumed name in 1845 and established Tubou dynasty. Converted to Christianity, unified the various feuding tribes and finally granted a constitution to his people.*

SALOTE (1900-    )—*Ruling Queen of Tonga. Her charm attracted world-wide attention when she attended the coronation of Queen Elizabeth in June 1953.*

EUGENE HENRI PAUL GAUGUIN (1848-1903)—*French painter, who went to the South Seas in 1890, later died there. He is best known for his paintings of the Tahitian people and landscape.*

ROBERT LOUIS BALFOUR STEVENSON (1850-1894)—*Scottish author who settled in Samoa. Best known works include* Treasure Island, Kidnapped, Dr. Jekyll and Mr. Hyde.

PIERRE LOTI (1850-1923)—*French naval officer and novelist. Wrote extensively about the Orient and South Seas. His books include* Le Mariage de Loti.

WILLIAM SOMERSET MAUGHAM (1874-    )—*English novelist and playwright. Used South Seas background for story of Sadie Thompson and* The Moon and Sixpence.

NORDHOFF AND HALL: James Norman Hall (1887-1951)—*American writer (resident in Tahiti from 1920), and* Charles Bernard Nordhoff (1887-1947)—*English writer, co-authored* Mutiny on the Bounty.

EDGAR LEETEG (?-1953)—*Artist who came to Mooréa and became internationally famous for his paintings on black velvet.*

HAROLD GATTY (1903-1957)—*Australian businessman and flyer. Established Fiji Airways and introduced tuna canning industry to South Pacific.*

JAMES A. MICHENER (1907-    )—*American author of Pulitzer prize-winning* Tales of the South Pacific, *and the novel* Hawaii.

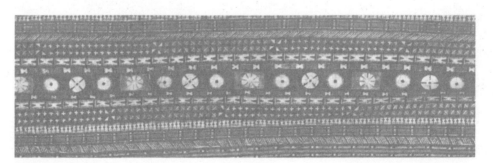

# SOME IMPORTANT DATES IN SOUTH SEAS HISTORY

*TONGA*

| | |
|---|---|
| 1616 | *Dutch navigators discover one of the islands.* |
| 1773, 1777 | *Captain James Cook visits Tonga, which he calls the Friendly Islands.* |
| 1822 | *First Wesleyan missionaries land.* |
| 1845 | *King George Tubou I, converted by missionaries, becomes sovereign and grants constitution to his people.* |
| 1900 | *Treaty of friendship between United Kingdom and Tonga.* |
| 1918 | *Queen Salote Tubou ascends the throne.* |

*FIJI*

| | |
|---|---|
| 1643 | *The Fiji Islands are discovered by Dutch explorer Abel Tasman.* |
| 1835 | *Reverend William Cross and Reverend David Cargill arrive in Fiji to introduce Christianity and abolish cannibalism.* |
| 1854 | *Thakombau, a leading chief, converts to Christianity and orders the practice of cannibalism given up.* |
| 1874 | *Native chiefs cede islands to Great Britain.* |
| 1879 | *Immigration from India begins; thousands are imported to work on sugar plantations.* |

*AMERICAN SAMOA*

| | |
|---|---|
| 1768 | *French explorer Bougainville visits Samoa.* |
| 1899 | *Under Treaty of Berlin, U. S. given rights to Eastern Samoa, Germany given rights to Western Samoa.* |
| April 17, 1900 | *Samoan chiefs sign Instrument of Cession with U.S. Flag Day becomes national holiday.* |
| 1951 | *Department of Interior takes over administration from Navy.* |

*WESTERN SAMOA*

| | |
|---|---|
| 1914 | *German administration replaced by New Zealand forces in World War I.* |
| 1919 | *League of Nations grants New Zealand a mandate.* |
| 1946 | *U. N. trusteeship administered by New Zealand.* |
| 1962 | *Western Samoa becomes fully independent.* |

*TAHITI*

| | |
|---|---|
| 1767 | *Captain Wallis discovers Tahiti.* |
| 1768 | *Louis de Bougainville takes formal possession of Tahiti for the French.* |
| 1769 | *British Royal Society sends scientific expedition under Captain Cook, who names group Society Islands in honor of his sponsor.* |
| 1788 | *Captain Bligh anchors* Bounty *at Tahiti. Stays five months collecting breadfruit plants to be taken to West Indies.* |
| 1797 | *London Missionary Society establishes headquarters in Tahiti for evangelical work throughout Eastern Polynesia.* |
| 1836 | *French Roman Catholic missionaries come to Tahiti, but are driven out.* |
| 1842-1843 | *France demands rights to visit island freely. Forces Queen Pomare to sign document giving France protectorate over Tahiti.* |
| 1880 | *Tahiti is changed from protectorate to French colony.* |
| 1914 | *German battle cruisers,* Scharnhorst *and* Gneisenau *bombard Papeete in World War I.* |
| 1940 | *Tahiti joins New Caledonia on the side of General de Gaulle and the Free French in World War II.* |

# SOME WORDS AND PHRASES FOR THE SOUTH SEA ISLANDS

| ENGLISH | FIJIAN | TAHITIAN | SAMOAN |
|---|---|---|---|
| Hello. | veikidavaka (*vay-kee-dah-*vah-*kah*) | ia orana (*ee-ah oh-*rah-*nah*) | ta alofa (*tah ah-*loh-*fah*) |
| Good-bye. | sa moce (*sah* moh-*theh*) | parahi (*pah-*rah-*hee*) | soifua (*soy-*foo-*ah*) |
| Please. | ni yalovinaka ka (*nee yah-loh-vee-*nah-*kah kah*) | i'au (*ee-*ah-*oo*) | fa' amolemole (*fah ah-moh-leh-moh-leh*) |
| Thank you. | vakavinavinaka (*vah-kah-vee-nah-vee-*nah-*kah*) | mauruuru roa (*moh-oo-roo-oo-roo* roh-*ah*) | fa' afeta'i (*fah ah-feh-*tah-*ee*) |
| I do not understand. | au sa sega ni kila (*ah-oo sah seh-ngah nee kee-*lah) | aita i papu ia'u (*ah-ee-*tah *ee pah-*poo *ee-ah-oo*) | le'i iloa (*leh-ee ee-loh-ah*) |
| May I take your picture? | laiva taba? (*lah-ee-vah tah-bah*) | e pata vau ito oe hohoa? (*eh* pah-*tah vow* ee-*toh* oh-*eh hoh-*hoh-*ah*) | pe e tusa ona pu'eata? (*peh eh* too-*sah oh-nah poo-eh-ah-tah*) |
| How much does it cost? | cava i voli? (*kah-vah ee voh-lee*) | ehia moni te'ie? (*eh-*ee-*ah moh-*nee *teh-*ee-*eh*) | efia le totogi o le mea? (*eh-fee-ah leh toh-toh-ngee oh leh meh-ah*) |
| House | vale (*vah-leh*) | fare (fah-*reh*) | fale (fah-*leh*) |
| Flower | se nikau (*seh nee-kow*) | tiare (*tee-*ah-*reh*) | fuga (foo-*ngah*) |
| Car, Bus | motoka (*moh-toh-kah*) | pereo'o (*peh-reh-*oh-*oh*) | fata (*fah-tah*) |
| Ship | sitima (*see-tee-mah*) | p̈ahi (pah-*hee*) | va'a (*vah-ah*) |
| Dance | meke (*meh-keh*) | ori (oh-*ree*) | siva (*see-vah*) |
| Loincloth | malo (*mah-loh*) | pareu (*pah-*reh-*oo*) | lava-lava (*lah-vah-lah-vah*) |
| Water | wai (*vah-ee*) | pape (pah-*peh*) | vai (*vah-ee*) |
| Beach | baravi (*mbah-rah-vee*) | tahatai (*tah-hah-*tah-*ee*) | 'auva'a ('*ah-oo-vah-ah*) |
| Man | tagane (*tah-ngah-neh*) | tane (tah-*neh*) | tagata (*tah-ngah-tah*) |
| Woman | yalewa (*yah-leh-vah*) | vahine (*vah-*hee-*neh*) | fafine (*fah-fee-neh*) |
| Love | loloma (*loh-loh-mah*) | here (heh-*reh*) | alofa (*ah-loh-fah*) |
| Day | siga (see-*ngah*) | ao (ah-*oh*) | ao (*ah-oh*) |
| Night | bogi (*boh-nghee*) | po (*poh*) | po (*poh*) |
| Today | e daidai (*eh ndye-ndye*) | te'ie ao (*teh-*ee-*eh* ah-*oh*) | asonei (*ah-soh-neh-ee*) |
| Yesterday | e na noa (*eh nah noh-ah*) | inanahi (*ee-nah-nah-ee*) | ananafi (*ah-nah-nah-fee*) |
| Tomorrow | e na mataka (*eh nah mah-tah-kah*) | ananahi (*ah-nah-nah-ee*) | taeao (*tah-eh-ah-oh*) |

### MONEY

| | |
|---|---|
| Tahiti | Tahitian franc |
| American Samoa | U. S. currency |
| Western Samoa | New Zealand pound |
| Tonga | Australian pound |
| Fiji | Australian pound |

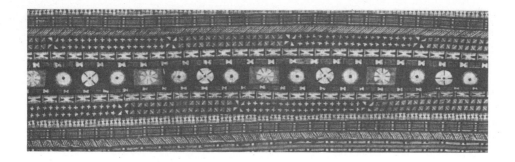

## INDEX